Practical Poetry on Slaying Dragons

by

Sherry L. May

ISBN: 0-75966-483-8

This book is printed on acid free paper.

1stBooks - rev. 09/20/01

Acknowledgements:

Thank you God for the gift!

Cover illustrated by Carlyn Kiehl.

Special thanks to my friend, mentor
and editor, Patricia Butin.

Thank you Dr. Adams, Dr. Polgreen, Dr. Chan.

Special thank you to Fred Capers for getting myself and
company to poetry destinations.

Thank you to those fellow dragon slayers.

Thank you Lisa for your tolerance of my confusion.

Dedication:

Thank you Mom for believing in me. Thank you God for my sense of humor.

TABLE OF CONTENTS

Inspiration For The Depression Dragon

I was attempting to clean my home and realized I was encircled by piles of clothes, books and other miscellaneous stuff.

I sat in that circle of stuff and cried. I felt so much darkness around me. I couldn't find my to do list and I couldn't remember where it all went. I was so lost and then, anger! I threw things all over the living room and I screamed! "Body! All my life I fought for you and you betrayed me! You let the mind go bad!"—I am a stroke survivor!

It was then I knew I was in the depths of Hell! I wrote the poem, The Depression Dragon that night and poems have been coming out ever since.

This poem won awards through the Famous Poets of Hollywood, the Diamond Homer Award, and A Poet Of The year, 1999. Because of that award, I had the chance to travel to Reno, Nevada, with my friend and mentor Patricia Butin and the opportunity to meet poets from all over the country.

The Depression Dragon

He comes roaring in with
Smoke and Fire
Takes away all desire of
accomplishing anything today!
All ambitions burned away!
You say to him "I hate you".
But, hate is too strong of word.
Because, in order to slay the dragon away.
At times you must embrace him.
Singed by his fire, choked by his smoke,
Say "I love you," to yourself and get up
To move around, there's no room for him to
stay, therefore,
He'll have to go away! The dragon has
been slain for that day!
Be proud YOU made him go away!
Hooray you Saved The Day!!!

Comments For The Depression Dragon

This poem I can say detoured a suicide. I had sent a copy to a pen pal who had gone into a deep depression and was considering suicide. He wrote to me that he had reread my poem and he is till writing to me!—Poetry can be helpful. After I had my stroke, I couldn't speak very well, so I read poetry aloud. It made me enunciate the words. It was my favorite face exercise! My favorite poem to read was "Still I Rise" by Maya Angelou. With every reading, I was battling to come forward out of the darkness that surrounds me. I still battle on a daily basis.—I hope and pray that this poem lets people know that life can and will get better. After all, life is about choices!

Inspiration For Dawn Marie

I have to go back to Branson! In between my moves from Branson and Iowa, I mourned the death of a cousin I had grown up with. Her name was Dawn Marie Harris and she had cerebral palsy. She had been in a wheelchair as long as I remember.

Before my stroke, since I was a young girl, I had visions and dreams. Now, I was sitting in my home in Branson. There was a cool breeze and light entered the room! It was Dawn and she was pirouetting in my living room! She was radiant. She gave me this poem and I wrote it down. After I had written the last word, she pirouetted down the hall, said "See you later!" and was gone. At that moment I understood why I was back here.

I called my Aunt, (Dawn's mother) and my mom at their catering shop in Iowa. They had just been discussing all the things Dawn could do now that she couldn't do when she was alive. I read them my poem and in tears, we all agreed she would be missed but she no longer had to deal with her pain.

This poem was read at Dawn Marie's funeral.

Dawn Marie

My name is Dawn Marie.
Please don't mourn for me.
I touched the lives that I was meant to
Now my job on earth is through!
God has called me home
Where I can run and I can roam!
I have a brand new body!
I can dance, laugh and play!
In this angelic body I will stay!

I'm alive! I'm alive!
Not just on the inside!
But in this angelic body
I can take some pride.
Walking, talking, laughing with my Lord,
I can even sing with all accord!
I am whole as never before,
In Heaven with my Lord!

Finally, I am free!

Inspiration For Circling

I was going to what I thought was my last trip to the Iowa City University Hospitals and Clinics. More brain tests! I call them 'the stupid tests', because you've known the answers before but you just can't access that information now. Therefore, you feel stupid.—

However, the people giving the test explain "Your brain is just slower. It's been severely wounded." This would not be my last visit.

Because I can't take my brain out and show the wounds, people have a tendency to say "You are okay physically. You are okay."

This poem describes what people cannot see that is happening inside to me!

Circling

On the outside I seem okay.
In my mind it's circling away.
Circling!
This circling inside my mind.
I'm tired of it all the time!
Nothing's where it's supposed to be.
So many times it's hard to believe
what I see! It can be very scary!
I want out of this dizzy ride!
I'm tired of the confusion always
inside! I battle hard to keep my pride!
Trying to stop the circling in my mind!
All the time struggling to find
    Peace of Mind!

Inspiration For The Beauty Is My Back Yard

This is one of my first poems. I thought that after Branson, the beauty was gone from my life forever, except for Missy. She was the Sheltie dog my mom and stepfather had gotten when I moved in with them. What I describe in the poem happened every morning. It gave me a reason to get out of bed!—

This poem won "An Editor's Choice Award 2000" presented by Poetry.com and The International Library Of Poetry. It was published in *America At The Millennium: The Best Poets of the 20th Century* anthology, 2000.

With this award, I knew it wasn't a fluke. There was something there!

The Beauty Is My Back Yard

I sit on the deck quietly to admire
The beauty in my back yard.

Mr. Squirrel comes down out of the tree
Where is the dog Missy? He wants to see!

Mr. Blue Jay perched on the fence!
For a morsel of food he'll wait hence.

Missy she chases the squirrel, Mr. Blue Jay
swoops in a whirl the morsel of food in his beak
does prevent him to speak, not a thank you
or anything but later he'll be back to sing.

They all know their role in the yard.
They don't even make it hard.
If only humans could be like the beauty
in my back yard.
Then life wouldn't be so hard.

Inspiration For Pride And Dignity

I was able to go to camp. A week at a brain injured camp. I was grateful for it, but I felt I was treated different there because I didn't need a wheelchair anymore, except for long distances. I didn't drag my leg when I walked. I worked very hard to not do these things. It had taken me a few years. It had taken an investment of time from friends and family. And, a lot of encouragement, which is what brain injureds aren't always given. Especially when it's easier to back their wheelchairs against a wall so they will not tip over! That's the time to get them out of the chair and into rehabilitation or a swimming pool. Or, they may use their legs to push their chairs backwards when what they really need is to be gently guided forward.

When you are a brain injured person, people tend to talk to you as though you know nothing. Unless you were brain injured as a child, you may not know anything. But, as an adult with a brain injury, you are an adult who is smart.

So please, do not patronize us. Do not speak to us in baby talk. You may have to speak slower, or repeat yourself several times, but please, do not treat us as if we were stupid!

It was because of my experiences at this camp that I was able to write 'Pride and Dignity'.—

Pride and Dignity

Is it too much to ask for? If anything,—it's all we have left!
All we ask is to be covered when we are bare!
Put yourself in our shoes and think!
What if that was me in that chair?
How would I feel in a big cold room—bare butted as can be!
A sheet or towel will do.
When left naked in a room,
vulnerable is what we feel, more than
we already are.
To sit in a chair for a day, please lift our
bottom to shift the other way.
We may not have the ability to speak.
We can hear you talk about our physic.
We cannot tell you loud and clear
what is wrong!
Look at our face, our eyes and you should know if we are happy
or sad. Even we can get mad. We are frustrated.
What seems to be a 'simple task'
we cannot do, like tying a shoe!
Inside these bodies there is a mind
That holds all of our Pride and Dignity.
If we could speak, we'd say please
            give it back to me!

Inspiration For Poem Of Peace

I have always felt that if you put women in charge of war, there wouldn't be any. Because a Mom would point out that there is no difference between the two of you. And that's how I came up with my poem of peace.

It flew into the mountains on "The Wings of Pegasus" in Reno, Nevada. It was great! A jazz band led the poets out with environmentally friendly balloons. *Oh When the Saints Go Marching In* was being played by the New Orleans band. I couldn't even have dreamt this for me.

The whole time I was there in Reno, all I could think of was 'I'm going to die before this is over!' It seems I was having an allergic reaction to a new medication, prescribed for me before leaving for Reno.

But I did manage to enjoy meeting people there. I may not remember names, but they all touched me deeply.

Poem of Peace

If I could see you and
you could see me

The same as each other
we would be.

To sit down and talk
like brother to brother,
Peace we could have like
no other!

Inspiration For Reflection

I was up at 4 a.m., reflecting on how lucky I was to be here and to have the privilege of meeting so many poets. To be given so many friends, to be given a gift to write out how I feel, even if I can't express that so clearly in speaking it.

What a wonderful opportunity!

Reflection

"One day at a time".
It's all we are given.
We have already had our
yesterdays, hope we used
them in the right ways!

Tomorrow's not here yet.
Use it wisely so we have—no regrets!

Today is the day to
use in kind. It's all
we have. "One day at a time".

Inspiration For Morning Rush Hour

I wrote this poem as my heart broke for these two women, who were ignored and left for dead. Separate incidents in a month. One lady had been thrown from a vehicle onto the Interstate. She had been run over so many times they couldn't even tell if she was a male or female until the autopsy.

The other was an elderly lady who was outside her apartment along the walkway, lying on the ground. How many passed her by?

Morning Rush Hour

Morning Rush, no time to stop
How many passed her by?
As she lay dying, then dead.
How many passed her?
As she anonymously slipped away,
How many passed her?

It only took one person to stop and say, I'm going
to see if I can help and then be on my way.
A human, not an animal on the ground, she did lay
No one said, "Who is it or what is it?" No, just
in a hurry!
How many passed her by?

We are such a numbed insensitive lot! You can almost
hear God crying. As she lay dying, then dead!

How many passed her?

Inspiration For A True Survivor

At the time of writing this book, we now have a young lady who was trapped in her car for five days! She had an accident and had gone into a ravine on the side of the road. Luckily, she was found, still alive, by a highway maintenance worker.

Why five days? Because people don't look around. Not even to admire what's around them. Just in a hurry to earn that almighty dollar.

Because people live so far out of their means, that they may not make it. I have had to learn to live slower and within one paycheck because of a stroke at thirty-five..

I now wonder, what did I miss? Who did I pass by? How big of a rush was I in before my stroke? Not too much, I hope. Sad that it took a stroke for me to see Life!

The young lady is alive and doing well, even though she lost both legs below the knees and had two broken arms. She graduated from high school as a Hero to her classmates and they gave a donation toward her new legs.—
Her GOAL is to walk again!

A True Survivor

(To be read with ATTITUDE)

So what you ate rats and slugs?
For five days she drank creek—water mixed with mud!

Oh, no blankys on the island
you didn't have!
She hardly had anything and
didn't go mad!

Five days there, both arms broken,
Legs gone below the knees!
I'd say she deserves the 'immunity'!

LINDSAY, LINDSAY, LINDSAY!

If anyone deserves a 'Survivor—Trophy', to me it is Lindsay!

Comments For A true Survivor

There are shows on TV where people think they have truly survived something out of their element. To me, Lindsay is a true survivor. Missing, but found alive, trapped in her car, after five days.

Donations toward Lindsay's medical bills can be sent to any Wells Fargo Bank in the country, in care of the Lindsay Thomas Fund.

Thank you!

Inspiration For I Cry For The Children

This poem was inspired by so much and so many! Ms. Oprah and all of the school shootings! I agree with Ms. Oprah. "Anytime there are children involved, I cry"!

I had been watching all of the news about the school shootings. I would cry!

If I was a parent, I would really pay attention to what my child was doing. I know it is hard out there. But becoming a parent is a big responsibility!

I understand it doesn't stop just because your child learns to walk and talk. It is a lifetime commitment. I think this is a part of our problem. A child needs guidance throughout their life. Not just 'Spot Checks'.

I Cry For The Children

All the shootings break my heart
Hungry children tears me apart.
I cry for the children.

They are supposed to feel safe!
To be safe! To hold their innocence
today they can hardly keep.
I get so angry at those creeps!
I cry for the children!

They are our future, an empty cup
to be filled with laughter and light,
to do this, we must treat them right!

I cry for the children!

Comments For I Cry For The Children

I was visiting my best friend Lisa, mother of my godsons. Jesse Dean is only five years old. Many things I don't remember and yet this is one thing I can't forget! He only goes to a very small rural school, a place you'd think he would be safe!

He came home with a note from the school. It read that a student had a gun in his backpack and was removed from the area! Lisa and I cried. I told her that I am not a mom, but I feel as if my chest has been ripped open and my heart is exposed! Lisa said that is what it feels like. I was relieved, angry, and trying to calm Lisa. She mentioned home schooling. I told her that you are not safe anywhere.

You just have to think safety! The age of innocence is dead! It is no more! Sad as it is.—
All we have is our faith.

Inspiration For Escape

I wrote this after the news. I don't remember where this happened. But, it was a story of a 32 year old man who had gone to an 18 year old girl and professed his love. She in turn was just a friend. He seemed to accept this and left the church. He returned, shot her, her mother, an innocent bystander, the minister and himself!

It stirred old memories for me.

Escape

He said if I can't have you, I'd rather see you—Dead! That's
what he said, that's what he said!

Through the beatings, then the rapes—you'd wish you were
dead! You'd wish he was dead! This is not my thinking. That's
what she said! That's what she said!

Must Escape! Must get away, to plan, to wait,
to Escape! Will he find me again? 'Not this time!' she said. **'Not
this time!'** she said. I'll do what I have to and I'll be hid! I'll be
hid!

At the beginning, trust no one!
Or I'll be dead! Yes I'll be dead!
You can not ever let your guard down!
Or you'll be dead, yes, you'll be dead!

The horror! The horror! To live
in this dread! To be in this dread
constantly within your head!

Sherry L. May

Inspiration For I Love Rain

I wrote this during an Iowa Spring rain!

I Love Rain

I love rain as it comes
down. It makes such
a relaxing sound.

The thunder a booming
sound as though it's
keeping the
rain gathered round!

The lightening flashes to show
it the way, where the rain
should fall for the day.

I love the Rain!

Sherry L. May

Inspiration For Mother Nature's Break

I wrote this on a glorious Fall day. Crisp and ready for the first snowfall. A Fall day in Iowa.

Mother Nature's Break

Mother Nature is preparing for her rest.
As a proud mother, she stands back to preview
Her harvest of Summer work. Deep reds,
Yellows, oranges and majestic greens. As
They fade away and carpet the forest floor,
She waits for there to be no more. So she—may cover the land
with its downy white
quilt. To let it rest, as she does, in her
Winter sleep. As she anticipates, to educe—the brilliant colors of
Spring.
To start her journey again!

Sherry L. May

Inspiration For Where Have The Morals Gone?

I wrote this after the news and feeling sad and frustrated because there were animals being treated badly with children and women being killed.

Where Have The Morals Gone?

Where have our morals gone?
It's open season on women and children!

So sad to hear, you can get more
time for killing an animal,
than you can a woman or child!

There are no morals any more!
I watched the news and the—World's gone wild!

Sherry L. May

End Times

I believe we are in the End Times and
God's love should shine!

Children are dying in the streets.
If not by a bullet, by not enough to eat!

Fuel is costing an arm and a leg!
Can we afford it on our wage?

Sex and violence everywhere! People
Pretending, they just don't care.

When we should be saying
How dare they? How dare they?
How dare!

Inspiration For Body Bags

My Mom and I had gone to Washington, D.C. to a poetry convention. What I saw broke my heart. It is a beautiful city with a desperate problem.

People were sleeping under the statues. We went on a trolley ride into the downtown area. I looked down the street and saw homeless people wrapped in plastic because of the rain. They lined the sidewalks for two blocks.

When I was crying Mom asked "Why are you crying?". I said "Look around, we are in what is considered the wealthiest country in the world. We are in the richest city and all of these people are sleeping on the streets. This is what you expect to see in Third World countries."

I was also embarrassed because of the people from other countries on the trolley.—

I was also ashamed.

Sherry L. May

Body Bags

A friend of mine said, tour D.C. by night!
We did. What an awesome sight, grand
building and all. At Lincoln's feet you feel
so small. And the cemetery stones a ghostly
white. It was a silent moment, what a cost.
The young men and women we have lost!
The downtown. What's that rolled in
plastic? Not a safe place to leave new
carpet! Wait! It's a tuft of hair, not—carpet! LOOK! Body Bags
of people, all lined
up. A shoe, an arm, a tuft of hair!
Sleeping on the concrete! I cried, "Doesn't
our government care?"
No they're not dead, walking corpses you see.
For they lost hope. They've lost their
dreams! They may as well be in body bags it—seems.

Comments For Body Bags

Instead of giving money to the panhandlers, ask the question How can I help you? I want to help you! And be ready to do so! Just like that saying, "Give a man a fish, he eats for a day. Teach a man to fish, he eats for a lifetime."

I myself would rather have life than just a day!

This poem received the Editor's Choice from the International Library.com, picked from 3.1 million submissions. Not bad.

Inspiration For The Awesome Ones

This poem came to me in song. It is the first poem in song. I was praying for some friends and this came to me. It was very beautiful.

The great thing is, I was able to hear my friend Lisa sing this in her angelic voice! It was the voice I had heard when receiving the poem.

The Awesome Ones

(Prayer Song For Women)

Thank You God for
Making us the Awesome ones!

Thank You God for—Making us the Awesome Ones!

You gave us strength to
persevere and courage from
Within here (point to heart)!

Thank You God for—making us the Awesome Ones!

(Repeat)

You chose us to be strong.
With the ability to give You a Son!

Thank You God for
making us the Awesome Ones!

The Awesome Ones!

Sherry L. May

A Hug

When I want a hug,
I just fill my bathtub.

Warm water and bubbles
Hug away my troubles.

I am hugged, totally, unconditionally.
A total body hug!

I get it from my tub!
Just a rub-a-dub-dub!!!

Inspiration For Slipping Into Darkness

I wrote this poem for my Aunt Shirley who is going blind from diabetes and glaucoma. She was the reason we kept in touch to know how our dad was.

I want her to know that I am forever grateful.

Sherry L. May

Slipping Into Darkness

Slipping into darkness
How scary that must be!
To know there will come a day
When you will never see!

Just remember all the sunsets,
sunrises and people that you love.
And always remember to trust in God above!
Even in the darkest you're never
alone. You have angels
around you, Joey, Patti, Kim and YaVonne.
They'll see that you'll carry on.

You see even in the darkness you're
never alone, always surrounded
by people you love.

My Spirit

My spirit has traveled many places.
Physically I have not gone and yet
As my spirit traveled I gathered knowledge
That made my soul so strong.
I also know the spirit—lives on and on and on....

Rebirth

Explosion in my brain!
Into a coma like back in the womb!
Awakened from the coma weak!

Like a newborn drooling and wetting myself!
Like a toddler, crawling, standing, falling,
walking! Like a child gently guided on your
way. Like a teen unsure of decision making!
Like a young adult out there and unsure!

I have been through a total rebirth!

TBI survivor

Inspiration For In Memory Of Kimberly

My original best friend was my sister Kim. She was sick most of her life and when she died of liver disease, a part of me went with her. I was sixteen and I became much older. I still miss her very much to this day.

In Memory Of Kimberly

(1996) 25 years ago you went away.
Never to come back that day.

Constantly thought of and missed.
It's now God's check you kiss!

You are lucky to be there.
We were lucky to have you here.

You are missed very much.
Many lives you did touch.

Thought of often until our end!
Daughter, Niece, Cousin, Sister, Friend.

We love and miss you, Kim!
September 5, 1962 - June 30, 1976.

Inspiration

Inspiration For Choices

I was anticipating sunrise. I was thinking about how I have been trying to explain to all my friends that you choose to be happy or sad!

Choices

Colors of grays and purples
Pinks and brightness.

It's choices how we color
Our world. Grays or beauty.

It's Choices! It's in Me!

Ho-hum is how some of us view—Our world, ourselves.

Think peacock! Kaleidoscope of color.
Surround yourselves with people of
Brightness and colors.

God will give you a rainbow!

Comment For Choices

I am unable to memorize my own work. This poem is sure proof of that. I received a letter asking permission to publish this poem. I told them they had put the wrong name on someone else's poem, because I could not find my original handwritten poem. I had misplaced a whole notebook.

I was embarrassed over that.

I would like people to see that we choose how to accept what happens to us. We can fight back, or accept and wallow in self-pity. I have chosen to fight back. It's called free will. Every one has it.

Note

Note

Note

Note

Note

Note

Note

Note

Note

Note

Note

Note

Note

Note

Note

Note

Note

Note

Note

Note

Note

Note

Note

Note

Note

Note

Note

Note

Note

Note

Note

Note

Note

Note

Note

Note

Note

Note

Note

Note

Note

Note

Note

Note

Note

Note

Note

Note

Note

About the Author

This is the part of who I am that led to this book!

My name is Sherry L. May. I was born and raised in Iowa, living briefly in Texas, Oklahoma and Missouri.

Following my dream, I was doing amateur Stand-Up Comedy when, at age 35, I had a massive hemorrhagic stroke. (I died during that stroke, but I came back.) I truly believe that I was made to come back for a reason. Actually, many reasons. The poetry I used to write, before the stroke, was to me very harsh.

Now, I see my poetry as softer and educating. I see life as lessons on looking at the world. This is how the world looks to me since I woke up from the coma, relearned how to walk, how to talk, and how to deal with life from a wheelchair. Now, I only use the chair to go long distances.

I have learned that people judge the brain injured very harshly because we can't put our brains in wheelchairs! I get angry and frustrated, and the depression is awful. I am a survivor, though, and if slaying the 'Dragons' of the world is why I am back, then so be it!

I really wasn't one for joining groups before, however my stroke has allowed it. I am now a member of two groups that you don't want to join. I am a Stroke Group Leader, affiliated with the American Heart Association. I am a member of the Iowa Brain Injury Association. And, I have recently been appointed to serve on the Iowa Governor's Brain Injury Advisory Board.

When I did stand-up comedy, I didn't even joke about politics. The closest I got to being politically correct was that I am vertically challenged. At 4 foot 11 in shoes, buying groceries has always been a challenge! My stroke has expanded my world.

www.ingramcontent.com/pod-product-compliance
Lightning Source LLC
Chambersburg PA
CBHW031314060726
47590CB00003B/1210